Songs of Distress

Abood's Anthology

Abdullah M

To those who feel.

(Not me trying to come up with something deep)

And also, to all those weathering the storms of emotions and distress.

Preface

It all started when I first gave poetry a chance and realised my love for writing, one thing led to another and here we are few years later where I've decided to finally share my work.

Songs of Distress is a collection of various poems written in a span of few years and conveys largely of different themes of human emotion. The different ways of how people express and experience various emotions in contrast to how I feel and express certain emotions. Emotions such as love and hate, joy and sorrow, hope and despair, and many other are expressed and portrayed in this book as themes. This book explores these topics in themes and guides raw emotions that hopefully can be related to or felt.

These emotions that are expressed are either based on real life instances, or a figment of my imagination or the byproduct of my experiences.

I hope that this book finds a way to resonate with your own experiences and stirs a deeper understanding within you and helps you navigate all your emotions.

Acknowledgement

Firstly, I would like to thank my mother who has always been very supportive of everything I do,

I would like to express my heartfelt gratitude to,

To my love,

To the readers and lovers of poetry,

To my friends and family,

To my publisher.

I offer my heartfelt gratitude for their support and encouragement and hereby present to you all with my book.

Introduction

In this anthology, we embark on a captivating journey through the kaleidoscope of emotions.

Each poem attempts to capture moments of vulnerability, resilience, longing, and transformation. Within it you will find bittersweet melodies of desire, notes of loneliness and an overwhelming presence of fear. Also woven throughout these poems, like a golden thread, is hope, a reminder that even in our most vulnerable moments, there is the potential for another chance and growth.

This anthology is a tribute to the complex human emotions and an invitation to embrace the full spectrum of our feelings and to navigate the depths of our hearts with courage and curiosity. Each poem, penned by a different emotion, adds a unique hue to this collective canvas, painting a portrait of the shared human experience.

May these poems resonate with your feelings and emotions and stir within you a deeper understanding of the intricate instances that shape your life.

\

Embark.

book
for
lost
souls

Book for Lost Souls

Lost souls travelling in the speed of light,

Finding it hard to express, the dark thoughts that come every night,

There exists a book, helping guide souls who've lost their way,

Giving them a map, instead of leading them astray.

A book written with tears, letting them face all their biggest fears,

A book that'll slowly fade away,

The lessons within always showing the way,

A book that's forgotten through the course of time,

A book with so much depth, doesn't even cost a dime.

Realising that the book for lost souls, is in fact just another lore carved in stones,

Providing them with false hope, temporary peace for lost souls,

Slowly turning their heart hollow, drifting through life with no purpose to follow,

A book for lost souls, a book filled with holes,

Lost soul with no goals, lost in between different roles.

Fool's
love

Fools love

Delayed but never late,

Holding you in my arms made it worth the wait,

A shrouded future lies ahead, hopeful and optimistic as we await,

Never smooth and easy, she painted a world with no hate.

She drives me crazy, blooming like the petals of a daisy,

Without her, everything around me seems hazy,

She came to me when I didn't need her,

A future without her, completely blurred,

Radiating an aura that can't be described with just one word.

No sins and sorrows, danced with her like there's no tomorrow,

Keeping my hopes high, like being on top of Kilimanjaro,

Realising that I'm at my best,

If it wasn't for you,

fools in love, only happens once in a few.

Lovesick
Nincompoop

Lovesick nincompoop

Even when I tried to hide my affection for you,

No matter how much I try I cannot subdue,

Your presence makes me feel like I'm in another dimension,

Making me think I'd do anything for your attention.

They say love is a thrill ride,

It's nothing as long as it's with you and for you,

Making me feel so entranced can't hide,

Overjoyed like a kid in a zoo.

I'm Addicted to the whole of you,

Coming back because I need more,

Feeling all trippy thinking of you,

This is just the beginning, waiting for what's in store.

Lavender

Lavender

Restlessness,

Agitation,

Anger,

Anxiety,

One glance at your lavender painted world and I'm at ease.

In this lavender painted sky,

A lavender girl with hazel eyes,

Moving so gracefully leading to my demise,

Can someone tell me, is she human or an angel sent from above?

An angel that could end my transgressions and cure my frosty heart,

Building our house with glimpses and pieces of that lavender aroma,

Slowing down time with that glittering smile,

Assured that indulging you is no bad for me,

The fragrance of your lavender lingers after indulgence,

Hoping that the scent won't fade away.

Clarity,

Contentment,

Elevation,

Happiness,

Love,

Resurrection of my frosty heart like that of a phoenix,

Activating my aura, the same way as smelling the scent of dried lavender,

Won't forgive us if you become a scent to remember.

caro
amico

Caro amico

Wish I could have realised about the way you were being treated earlier,

Acting like it's not a big deal and relentlessly becoming a Journeyer,

Rues of not saving the piece of you that's already dead inside,

Cognate thoughts and feelings of mine while you sat beside.

Say how-come you talk of this agony like all passable?

Yager to the chest believing that all this is unsurpassable,

Elusive thoughts on why you presume this scrap is yours alone to fight?

Daimyo protected by his samurai, protecting your heart from adversity I plight.

Do you wanna talk?

Am I bothering you?

Unacceptable and unforgivably alone you walk,

Misunderstandings and instances can't tarnish this bond that's left undue.

Wishing I could always be there for you don't you know that I'm always right here?

Hoping to forget the bad memories making them disappear,

An uppercut to make me think right again,

Reassuring standing with you-

Even after ten.

Ineffable
Infatuation

Ineffable infatuation

So, there was I, tolerating my vanilla way of living,

Being hopeful for something to transpire, cannot stay the same until I retire,

Wanting a place to seek refuge, someone to cover me as I perspire,

She provided, an abode, rapidly turning everything colourful, it feels surreal as he's slowly healing.

I still eye her with misgiving.

A notion of wanting all of her every day, wanting her forever,

An ineffable mystery, the kind of love you're so certain about,

Putting my all into it, working on us endlessly, same problems resurface no matter how much we endeavour,

As long as she's with me, we discover reasons to be together, as they sprout.

Hopeful that you don't turn into a memory, A memory that'll

Shut his heart forever,

He keeps himself alive by living through this memory,

A memory, so precious and bittersweet yet savoury,

Protects it from coming out of his heart, it's his treasury.

Ineffable infatuations, comes and goes, mine stays forever,

A memory that he'll never let go ever.

REFLECT.

tainted
trust

Tainted Trust

Standing there on the other side, eyes wide open as I see your actions decide,

Deciding the fate of our future, tainting it with distrust and suspicion,

Did it all for love, what we had would've been auspicious,

Broke the barrier, broke what held us together, now I'm always under the weather.

The world seems monochromatic and dull, you've taken my light away,

For old times' sake, just stay with me for one last day,

We can do everything we love, Except it won't the same,

A crime of passion, breaking my trust leading me to new ideas,

Inspiring me to prove you wrong, playing until there's no one to blame.

Said you'd rather be in hell than alone?

Tainting trust, nothing left to do but atone,

Reminiscing, thinking of everything whilst holding a cup of caffeine,

Thinking of what it could've been, tainted yet serene.

Relic

Relic

Been searching through this vast desert for a relic,

Amidst the barren and hostile sandy waves lies something angelic,

A commodity that merchants and maidens strive for before weathering,

But the desert is unforgiving and unbiased resulting-tethering.

Trying to break off the shackles to stop the dormancy,

Being subdued in the sandstorm pleading for mercy,

Once you flee the dry erosion there awaits vegetation,

A place in our mind that feels like a hut near a river basin.

Ample amounts of love and humility during irrigation,

Realisation that the relic you've been searching for is the gift of life,

A path with prudence gratitude one can attain salvation,

Adapting and navigation will help you in the time of strife.

Sirius

Sirius

She, an infinitesimal being,

Drifting through this vast galaxy unseen,

Led astray in the moon's shadow slowly creeping,

In search of that harmonic cosmos where all is serene.

She, an infinitesimal being,

Eludes from the supernova explosion scarcely,

He grasps her from peril, their meeting was unseeing,

An intertwining of stars which is rarely seen.

She, an infinitesimal being,

His heavenly body pulling her towards the centre,

Colliding against him, an inadvisable prospect for disaster increasing,

Likelihood of a stellar collision foreseeable, they surrender.

She, an infinitesimal being,

Realising that he is just an optical illusion,

A bright star distorting reality and wellbeing,

An interstellar union with penitence conclusion.

Between the notes
of love

Between Notes of Love

As I laze around between notes in a song,

Setting aside my calling the delay is long,

Longing for two wintertides as she made her intro,

It was as though she was meant for, took me over slow.

Her voice resembles the verses of a song sounding poesy,

Making me want to listen to her like a chorus made for me solely,

A humid Sunday night the tension was there,

Trying to create the bridge with her having no despair.

Like the shine of a rose quartz she stood within sight,

Desperate to win her with all my might,

The strings were tied, and a seal was all in all then came the disruption,

Looking at us stunned and speechless our night out came to a
conclusion.

Indescribable feelings and glimmering eyes she glanced,

Being with her had me put into a trance,

Certain that the love won't fade out,

Come closer give you all my love throughout.

27
june
27

June 27

June 27, she spears through the cloud covers,

her shiny Awezah flickering in his eyes,

feeling tangled up and blue hanging about to recover,

she purifies his heart with her laugh like he's been baptised.

June 27, the day passes by trying to get her out of his mind,

Cannot make it stop, he's possessed,

she stood before him partially reclined,

Pyrite in her arms in a trice she confessed.

June 27, three words making his mind feel entranced,

heart in his mouth running as he danced.

June 27, he will never let you go,

you are all he knows.

Six Scars

Six Scars

Everything heals, except for the scars that you've left on me,

Turning off the lights doesn't help me sleep, reflecting about everything I did,

Six scars slicing through my chest, trying to run off but can't flee,

Showing me the cold shoulder, grieving until there's swelling in my eyelid.

Six hours overthinking, constantly recollecting the same words,

Like the sounds from hummingbirds, her harmonics slit me into thirds,

Weakened by her resolve, kept prioritising her giving me more scars,

Rescuing myself because no one will, soothing my heart with stars and cigars.

Proclaiming that you need me, yet you find ways to drown me,

Drowning my feelings, a hollow heart with six battle scars,

Auctioning off my heart for solitude as I visit different bazaars.

Six scars, ones my drained mental.

Six scars, twos my foreboding future.

Six scars, threes my burning passion.

Six scars, fours my self-esteem.

Six scars, fives my love that I cannot redeem.

Sixth scar, took away my ability to dream.

Is it wrong of me to expect the same? It hurts but I'm still playing your game,

An itch on my scars every time you call my name,

Six scars, sixty scars, six hundred scars, your love for me will always be the same.

Transcendent
goddess

Transcendent Goddess

The night of the full moon,

The sunset of frore,

The Esperance rose of june,

The Shalimar gardens of lahore,

Whatever it is I profess,

You're more enticing.

The glamorous cherry blossoms of Hirano,

The pink sandy beaches of bermuda,

The enchanting vineyards of vulcano,

The vibrant and colourful streets of cuba,

Whatever it is I profess,

You're more enticing.

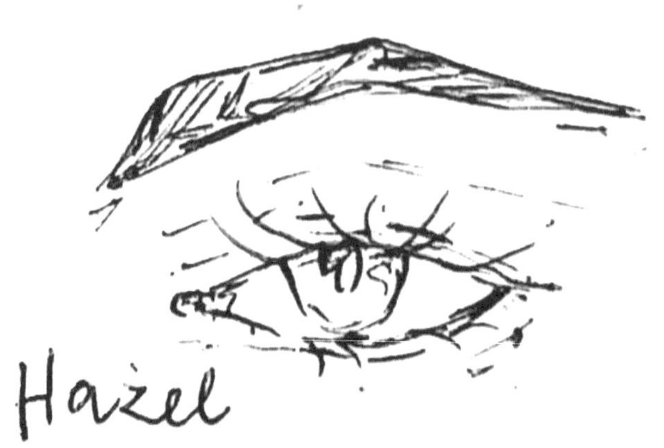

Hazel

Hazel

Brown eyes mesmerise,

Her radiating smile I memorize,

They say never trust the people you love,

Prepared to gamble and ready to fall from the skies above.

Looking at her gives me a quick rush of euphoria,

The same sentiments as indulging in glass wisteria,

Tell me, how can I evade such an enchantress?

Hitting me with an uppercut with all her might like a praying mantis.

She hits like ecstasy making me want more,

Sleepless nights thinking of her got me dreaming on the floor,

Living in a world where everything is illuminated by her,

The path is clear, the goal is near, what am I waiting for?

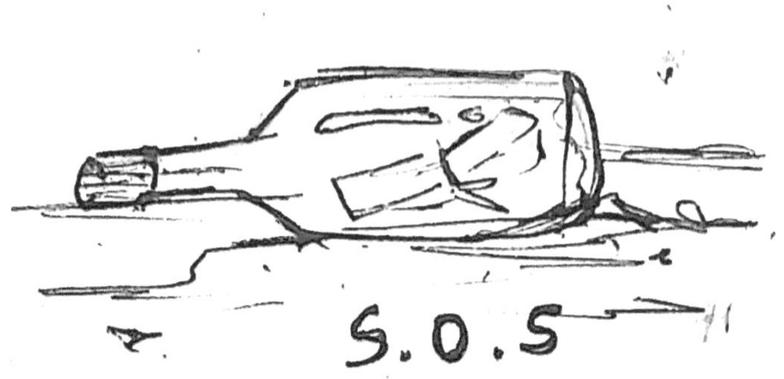

S.O.S

S.O.S

4 October 2022

This is a message from a bottle
If found please makesure it goes to her

Salvation, My life is in her hands,
Marooned and hopeless as I lay alive,
Finding a bottled message in these wavy sands,
Her absence slowly reduces my will to survive.

Without you, I am lost,
Forced to spend my life in misery,
Hoping my message of love reaches at all cost,
Then she comes gloriously,a single artillery.

With red shaded hair, full of stupidity,
She joins me on this rogue journey with no end,
Believing in our love as we full send,

Break the bottle, run towards me with full throttle,

We'll breeze past every gruesome huddle,

This is a throwback to the mud puddle,

Wake up! All this time we were in a cute cuddle.

DESCEND.

Let go, Let in

Let go, Let In

Been delaying the time to let go,

Kept holding me back, halting my flow,

Wanting me to be there for you,

never gave me a reason to,

Hung me up on your cross, contemplating if it were ever true.

Held you up when you were suffering,

Like the wings of a butterfly, went away fluttering,

Letting you go extinguished the burning flames within,

Pulling me into a void, still not ready to give in.

Recalling the end of a horrendous disaster,

Cannot surrender these memories, taking them with me to the hereafter,

Grateful that I stopped, didn't run past her,

She helps me heal, covering the wounds in plaster.

Hearts
Adytum

Hearts Adytum

At the conclusion of midsummer lies a fallen star,

Heart twingeing without her whilst holding a cigar,

She's waiting to fall in love But I'm ready,

Getting sucked into tophet she came and saved me like mehdi.

Dreaming of being alone as I lie awake,

Angelic as she was, loving her wasn't my biggest mistake,

Thought of losing you got me afraid again,

Struggling to stop being covetous as I hide in Vienne.

Taking the weight of my shoulders of distress,

Falling for her touch, Unable to escape nevertheless,

Sitting with my ashcan feeling saudade as I cuss,

Fantasising about us, just to get a glimpse of us.

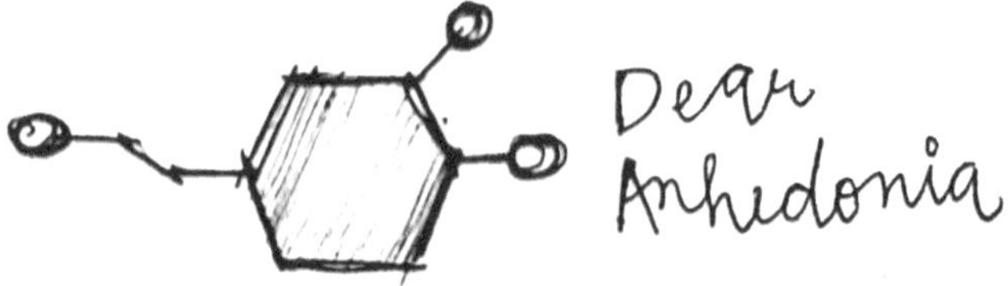
Dear
Anhedonia

Dear Anhedonia

Here I am, resting on my couch scrolling through my notes,

Feeling neglected as I recollect all these instances in hopes of,

Feeling it one more time, The love, The pain, Anger and desire,

Now it's just emptiness, flowing around detached in absence of any emotion.

Cloud spotting helped free my imagination, now it's meaningless,

Long naps and cuddles with you cured my heart, now her touch is pointless,

The groovy rhythms and melodies healed me, now I feel nothing from it,

Your love, it once gave me a reason, for my anhedonia it was treason.

Oxytocin, dopamine and serotonin, they used to make it all okay,

Struggling to fight back against it, I've been left to decay,

Realising I'm not the same as I was,

You're my only regret, wishing I could love you more as my end draws.

Here I am, whatever I am, The embodiment of my past self, The hollow knight with no soul,

Chemicals flowing within me with no role,

I once loved, now I'm lost, I can't cry even if I try,

Watching the birds fly, saying my last goodbye.

LISTEN.

Nostalgia

Nostalgia

As the day bleeds into nightfall,

Reminiscing and resting on a sidewall,

About the ludicrous memories we shared,

Spontaneous actions, going through it all unprepared.

The long conversations,

The pointless interventions,

The constant words of consolations,

The countless called off vacations.

These nostalgic memories, these thoughts making a mess of my mind,

A great deal of problems, we stuck together even in a bind,

Sometimes, wonder if everything was a repercussion of mine,

Or was it meant to be; we were never meant to entwine.

Nostalgia,

Is it a blessing or a curse?

The more I remember, the closer I get to my hearse,

Nostalgic memories, tinging through my spine,

There was a fine line, a sign, it was meant to decline.

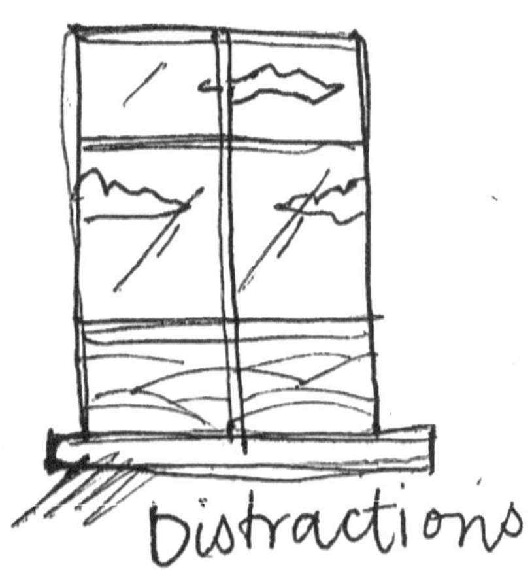

Distractions

Distractions

I see,

That distracted look of yours,

As you sit there and ruminate about your thoughts,

I wonder if there's something bothering you,

Staring at the endless golden sunset hue.

You seem stuck, A mind dwelling in polarized darkness,

A hearts distraction,

Have I shown myself hastily and full of curtness?

May sound absurd, I face them all and make amends,

Seeking help from me, trying to cope,

Deceiving distractions, making me believe I still got hope.

Even when you're out of my sight, you scurry your way into my mind,

Distractions, pondering about the way it was,

a good find,

you were so kind,

I was completely blind,

you kept my thoughts confined,

A love that'll always remind,

Distractions,

Trying to move on, it stays undetermined.

Love
lies

Love Lies

Don't look back, I'm slowly fading away,

Said what you said, led to my suffering yet another day,

You keep finding so many ways to put me in dismay,

You've blocked my flow, no point praying as I slowly decay.

Love lies, an eye for an eye, cry looking at the sky, unfavourable situations yet I still comply,

Putting my faith in you regardless of what anyone says,

Getting hurt is eventual every time she stays,

From the heavens above to the hells below you've put my happiness on delay.

Numerous times you've lifted me up just to put me down, humorous how there's so many different ways you've found to make me frown,

Kept you on the pedestal, gave you my crown,

All that just to put me on the ground, leave me to drown.

Tide after tide, floating endlessly through these thoughts,

Clotting my brain thinking as I try and undo the knots,

Lie to hide another lie,

desperate for your love lies as I stay dazed in bed.

Love lies, time flies, misled, misread, fled as you filled me with lead,

Love lies, the truth doesn't matter when you're already dead,

Loving your lies, love you like the blue skies.

INFECT.

Remember
me

Remember Me

Say, will you remember me after I'm gone?

Will you remember, the way he loved?

Or was he just, A part of her checkered chess board? A little pawn,

Only time will tell, for he spent moon over her, his beloved.

She chased for a feeling he always had in his heart,

Before she knew it, it all turned to dust, glittering hearts they were miles apart,

Regret and remorse all the mistakes, time that cannot come back,

Life will get better he said, returning back to his lonely shack.

His time had come, he was ready to succumb,

There she was, he looked down from above, what has she become, brittle and numb while choking on rum,

A face of someone bereaved, she spent the rest of her night in grieve,

She didn't want him to leave, he didn't have it in him to believe.

He wanted to reprieve her of her sorrows,

In order to achieve, he sacrificed all of his tomorrows,

Say, will you remember me?

Agree to disagree, her love for him has no degree.

Paralysed

Paralysed

Sinking into hebetude after taking a glance,

You and I, we were meant for something solid and perpetual,

In my heart of hearts yearning to give you another chance,

Agonisingly I squelch to prevent from anguish which was eventual.

I couldn't save us and now I bear weights of regret and prospect,

You've killed me from within I'm paralysed,

Losing selfhood gives rise to mortality in every aspect,

Being solitary doesn't mitigate a heart that's terrorized.

Some intoxicate the mind to open their hearts,

All a gimmick to cower from facing factuality,

Hoping that she removes the shackles of numbness and alleviate as it departs,

Leaving with all my faith as I return to normality.

Void

Void

Woke up next to the shore,

Aching as my chest feels tight,

These emotions are relentless can't take it anymore,

But no matter what it just feels right.

When one starts to disregard your thoughts and perspective,

You endure an emptiness overtaking your body,

It erratically makes you regret the efforts and halt wanting to be protective,

Forgive me, for I am not the best to embody.

Embodiment of being the best version of oneself,

A lie I tell myself every night,

You've created a void inside me all I did was love you more than I loved myself,

But alas life isn't seamless, at the end of the tunnel there is light.

The Beauty of a
Mud puddle

The Beauty of a Mud Puddle

Oh, great there's mud all over my shirt,

All when I was trying to be a flirt,

And as we walked, she looked at me with contempt,

It felt like winning her love was a failed attempt.

As I walked back towards the puddle,

It looked so good with sparkle and bubble,

I took of my shirt and took a leap,

I've got nothing to lose, in very deep.

As I sit in the puddle, took a glance at the sky,

Oh, my I've got groceries to buy,

I might buy a pint thinking about hadal,

Astagfirullah that's not halal .

(I don't condone drinking)

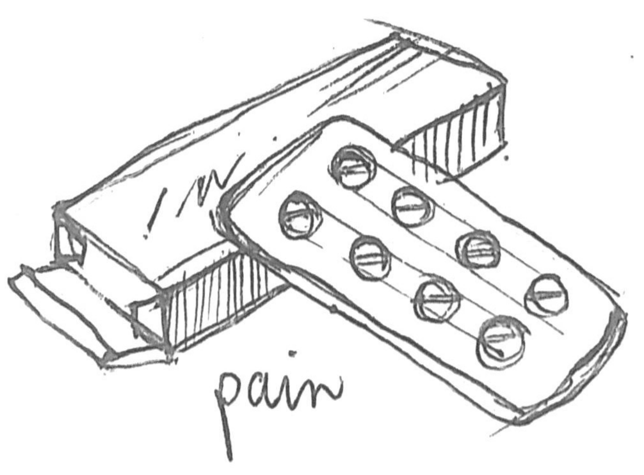
pain

Pain

What's this pain I feel in my chest,

Could it be because of the high cholesterol,

No, it can't be the agony is different,

What could put me in such misery,

Ever since the sunder I feel cold blooded,

Now I know the cause of this pain,

It's just a person with a shattered heart,

Sitting in oblivion one can recuperate.

silent
symphonies

Silent Symphonies

Come any closer, you can hear the silent symphonies,

Eerie and ghoulish, a world created by miserable epiphanies,

Help!

Slowly losing myself, twenty,

Showered me with your love, plenty.

The same love that helped, burn me in a hopeless dream,

Every night, she torments me in my dreams,

I yelp!

Over the hill, across the stream, been with you in any extreme,

Dealt with your problems, she took me to all extremes.

You reap what you sow,

Your silence says it all, that's all I needed to know,

Please help!

I never listen to the silence, it screams,

Always falling into that trap, same schemes .

Second
best

Second Best

A blue hearted girl that everyone admired,
Striving to be the one who kept her inspired,
That was until everything about her transpired,
Second best, she couldn't reach what was always desired.

Agitation and anxiousness kept her awake at night,
She wanted her light to shine bright,
Even on rainy days where it's all white,
She wanted to fight, no one could understand her quite.

Second best, she was miles above the rest,
Had it in her to overcome every quest,
The greed of being the best made her fail the test,
It was after all the simplest of tests, to live and love just like the rest.

The best, she stole her joy,
There was nothing left anymore for her to enjoy,
She wanted out, she had to destroy,
Second best, there's always another boy.

Stay
Away

Stay Away

Pushed me away, I was at the edge of my rope,

Accepting this fate whilst breaking my back as I cope,

No point in lying, been honest with you always,

Until hell freezes over, you've left me in the crossways.

Playing your game, playing only to lose,

Blinding me, blinded only when you're covering the views,

Pretending, pretending that it's all okay,

Wanting all of you, wanting you to stay.

Roles reversed, you wanted more and more,

Expecting me to put you out of your misery as I leave from the front door,

Stay away, away from me, done listening to your excuses,

Counting on me to stay, no point waiting, slowly turning grey.

Stay and suffer in silence,

poked a hole in the heart with a steel lance,

Ending it beautifully,

last chance, last dance.

past
Fantasized

Past Fantasized

Thought he was just like every other, A fantasy,

Standing there unmindful, she brought with her a duffel of agony,

Trauma of yore, her eyes revealed a reflecting Kagami,

Oh my, A past overfill of tragedy.

Her perception of love, unawareness of dangers, she lived in fragility,

Cautious little steps, avoiding torments in close proximity,

Finding a world void of toxicity, she grew with hostility,

All she ever wanted, was for him to fill her with affinity.

Her past, the only thing holding her back from dreaming,

Dreaming for rose petals and lilies,

Starry nights and big cities,

Dreaming of eventually, seeking love, feeling loved, leaning on whilst healing.

Her past, it transpired and was left unresolved,

He played a part in what was to befall,

Holding on to whatever was left of him, she revolved,

Past fantasized, it finally hit her like a brick wall

Austin's
woes

Austin's Woes

Another sabbath Twas I choking on a cigarette,
Respiring a cold breath feeling glacial perceiving silhouette,
Overthinking every circumstance failing to fall asleep at night,
Presuming that puffing can shelter me from her frostbite.

Keeping me wrapped around your finger I'm captivated,
A gaze from her putting the screws on-activated,
Promising to protect my heart like a sergeant,
Guillotine to my devotion forming an insurgent.

Mumbling her name and yearning for when she's not around,
Waiting with my Cuban for another heartbreak inbound,
I should've listened to them-didn't bother me too much,
Keeping the effort having no grudge.

The signs were visible overlooked it all,
Laughing by myself realising I deserved this fall,
Puffing a pack with regret as I recall,
Was her love real? I can't even bawl.

New beginnings

New Beginnings

The same old sun shining on a new day,

Giving rise to resolutions and shrine visits, we pray,

For a new beginning, a one unlike its predecessors, ending in dismay,

Hopeful for the scorching heat to not lead me astray.

An aura of hope, a symbol of change, a sign to start, something great and recall,

Fighting at any cost to break out of the cycle and experience,

To be ready for all challenges that come about, prepared to dive and freefall,

A calm mind, an open vessel, striving for greatness whilst being delirious.

New beginnings, same old shortcomings,

New bonds, same old taunts,

New love, same old shove,

New year, hopeful for something to not go wrong, same old fear.

Life

Life

She provides me with hurdles that make me stumble,

The boundless times you've brought me back after a fumble,

They say mountains and hills may crumble,

Life finds a way to unveil things, making you humble.

The Golden hour, a magical hour, where life begins and ends, a sight to witness,

Sometimes overflowing, finding ways to fill into an empty heart, whilst everything is in stillness,

Radiant glow, radiant heart, life gives a chance, to snicker away all your fears and flow,

This is your time, a small push forward, someone to stand behind and hear the prevailing chime.

Life, what a beautiful thing she is,

Giving and taking, playing with everything that was meant to be his,

An angel of light, blinded by her sight, what's life without a fight?

It was never right.

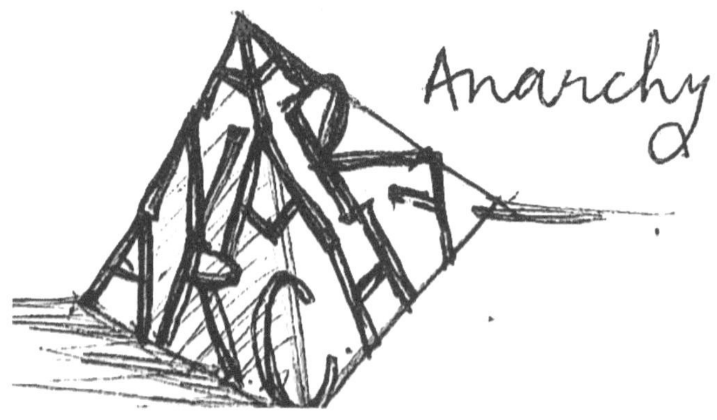

ANARCHY
Anarchy

Anarchy

Assume world nihil of adversity,

Nexus between citizenry and potentate will diminish,

Autarky for mortals would seem bliss,

Re-establishing being in the state of nirvana,

Calamity comes like Sakura's life span,

Hold on to your loved ones and shelter them,

Yearning forever for a world with no corners.

(What is bro cooking?)

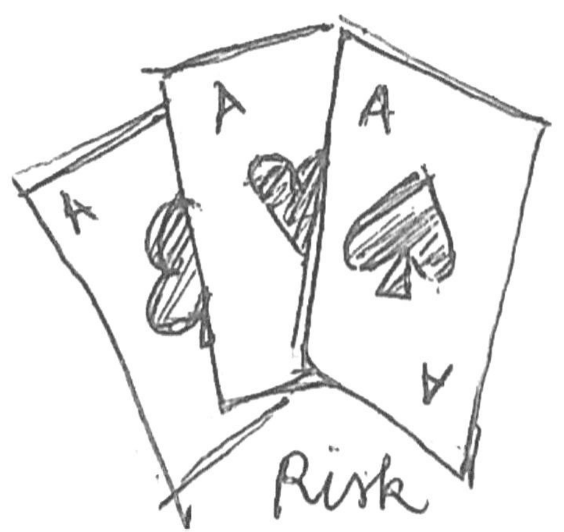

A
A
A
Risk

Risk?

Living life on edge,

Playing your cards and pushing me of the ledge,

Moments ponder could've saved us from all this backlash,

Ending with a barrier between us, there was no need to clash.

No risks, no rewards?

Playing my instrument with no chords,

Hearing everything you say but cannot comprehend,

Just walking away with no pain, we can all pretend.

Reaching the final valley together was our little fantasy,

You've erased the future, the past remains prominent and gratifying,

I bid adieu dear companion as I return from tragedy,

A beautiful tale, horrifying yet satisfying.

Negativ.

Negativ

Living life although not in the right direction,

Countless different phases like the recurring themed seasons,

Chained heart protecting itself from social rejection,

Dealing with these negative emotions as though they're heathens.

Why should I endure all this hate?

For I am innocent as a mockingbird,

Anger and apathy towering within, fearing it's too late,

Moments robbed, spiralling downwards clenching these negative emotions-Absurd!

A battle of the mind and soul we cross swords,

Down on my knees, you weren't there to appease,

Biding time for a resurrection filling agitation in hoards,

Revenge doesn't put your mind at ease.

Euthanasia
gastgedal

Euthanasia Gastgedal

She lays there lifeless but full of life,

Ironic during life she dwelled in agony,

Despaired life, losing touch, widowed wife,

Fighting chance life provides with to accompany.

Accompany to go on an exanimated life without being sotted,

She rests next to the ash-can unsatisfied with this life and its melancholy,

Behold came an angel administering her ruinous life-blotted,

life was sour another angel gone to waste-heavenly.

He hates it now that she's gone,

Despite the fact he aided her with euthanasia,

Happiest she's ever been with the start of a new dawn,

Brimming with life she burns in acacia.

(What's with the weird title's?)

War

War

As I stood with my fellow confrère in this sultriness,

Standing on the other side of the trench,

Our dearest of foes strafing at us with bitterness,

The theatre filled with ichor overfill of stench.

As we made it towards the entrance of the fort,

Vanquishment of der feind was nearing,

The commander gallops approaching us hurt,

Clasping him towards the citadel cheering.

He quaffed with us until his final twitch,

Writing a letter to his inamorata was unaccomplished,

The ether was pumped full of lead identical to an ignition switch,

As we laid him on the loam regardé perished.

Our loved ones yearning for a homecoming,

The smoke cleared the borough was nearby,

They clinched our bodies with doting,

Finding solace in rough seas.

Effet papillion

Effet papillion

There she stands very still on a cold arid night,

An inkling of being unsafe hoping no one's around in sight,

The gully brimming with darkness a stalker with heinous intent,

She just wants to slacken up go about her business feeling discontent.

The feeling of having butterflies in the stomach, is she truly free and independent?

When she isn't free to do whatever, she wants and be completely transcendent,

A province is truly free when she feels emancipated and unconfined,

In a place where she can explore with no bounds-people with freemind.

Are we truly freeing with all these shackles hanging on our neck like a pendant?

That feeling of butterflies leaving is excruciating but copendant,

But someday she could stroll about without worrying,

She greased her air force ones,

She needs to stop hurrying.

Double
Standards

Double Standards

I was there when you needed me the most,

I was there when you were at your lowest,

I was there to heal and grieve as you dosed,

I was there when your thoughts traveled the slowest.

Where were you when I needed you the most,

Tumbling down, shelter me before I reach my lowest,

Camped and cuddled next to the ashcan as I dosed,

Better off alone rather than being with you in my slowest.

complacent

Complacent

Finding ways to escape out of my mind,
Making things more complex, I'm running out of space,
Wasn't warned about the dangers feeling alone and confined,
Regretful as I was, being complacent made me lose your grace.

Realising that your love never really scared me,
Unaware of the demons that stopped me from dreaming,
Saying that leaving me behind is what set you free,
A painful situation to be in, never redeeming.

Taking pride in quick decisions, what can I say,
Skipping past questions and factors, A timebomb in delay,
Played with my heart, I was being too complacent,
A place in my heart, always in adjacent .

consolatio Munitum

Consolatio Munitum

All this time I've been hiding,

But when I was with you, I felt at ease.

Drinking a cup of coffee by the corner and writing,

About the way you flick your hair to appease.

Every so often I get the notion of taking you back to our latibule,

Where we can hear melodies and not worry about sorrow.

It's amusing the way you protected me from all the adversaries like a capsule,

You've moved on but I still yearn for that rendezvous tomorrow.

You and I will meet again,

It'll just be reminiscences this time.

soul
searching

Soul Searching

Now that I've withdrawn to my kingdom,

I'm all alone in this space escaping from reality,

Sitting in solitude attempting to solve my problems,

You've played with my feelings, my hearts a casualty,

Going through this same thing every night,

Striving to remove this addiction of needing you,

The path towards serenity is tough but bright,

Abandoning my solitude knowing I grew,

As I return back to reality feeling nervous,

I'm lost in the sound, can't seem to find my purpose,

I've won the battle but lost in Perth,

Starting all over again feels like a rebirth.

Hindered
Heart

Hindered Heart

Tuesday eve, down flat on my face,

Laying to forget, that captivating voice I've been meaning to erase,

The love we had is something that can't ever be replaced,

Your actions, your decisions, didn't consider my heart leaving it displaced.

Being so discreet and shady, nothing left for me to say,

Making me feel distrusted,

leaving me in dismay,

Shouldn't have ignored the cracks in the surface,

Took everything from me, feeling worthless.

Walked down the wrong way, been led astray,

My betrayed heart trembles with

disappointment while being on display,

Can someone take out these feelings, so it gives me more reasons,

I need some more reasons to live out these seasons.

The beginning of the end

Are you happy with how things are?

Some might say the end isn't too far,

Can someone be satisfied with what their given?

You're never happy no matter how much I give in.

Life tends to find a way to open and create new beginnings for us, we only realize the severity of anything when were in too deep, to a point of no return, that is when you question yourself,

Are you happy with how things are?

Do you have it in yourself to deal with the forthcomings and have a strong front.

We never know when it ends, or if it even began in the first place

Then comes the standard and satisfaction,

Are you okay with how things are?

Are you SATISFIED with this???

Is it really worth it, I say nay but there's a possibility of it being worse.

No one is ever happy with what they have, that's just how the world works,

You keep chasing, but hey at the (end) will you give in?

So much happening around us,

So many problems fond of us,

A lifetime to evade and try to need cause a fuss,

Sitting in deep thoughts, just missed my bus.

People take life and its moments for granted, regardless of it being good or bad.

Yeah, sure we all have a lot going on, but is it worth creating huge grievances and hassle to yourself and the people around you?

Relax!!

If you don't depart now, you may end up dealing with this throughout the entirety of your lifetime.

We don't need that now do we.

So much is happening around you, Souls in deeeep thoughts tend to miss the "NOW".

Why bother about something in the past, its history for a reason.

Learn and move on.

You don't want to stand in the scorching heat and wait for another bus now do we?

Half past six still trying to heal,

He didn't know a broken heart only needs time to heal,

A hot summer left out with nothing to feel,

Half past six, a broken heart that still wants to feel.

In a very fragile state,

All a person needs is time to comprehend and understand the situation.
the more time they take the better it will be to move past the calamity.

Yet we all stand and make our lives more miserable but not listening
and giving ourselves time. valuable untradeable time. if the heart is left
out to rot and dry, till probably losing emotions and the ability to feel.

A heart that's stone cold and yearns for something to feel,

Now that's something taken for granted.

The harder you try, the more you compromise,

This is just the beginning of the end, I promise,

Twelve months seems long, passes quick in vain,

Why does it always have to end in pain.

Why does it always have to be miserable?

Why frown, somethings just cannot be irreversible,

Why give them any moments joy?

You're not the same teenage boy.

Are you satisfied enough?

It's okay love, I know it's been rough,

It never really ends, it was all a bluff,

Darling, act tough, sometimes all we need is a puff.

Paint a wall of closure, write a book for closure, repercussion of repercussions for closure, honey this doesn't bring the end closer.

Where were you?

I needed you,

Said you'd be there in two,

Blindsided view, it was long overdue, if only I knew,

You were never true.

I begged and begged,

Why can't this end?

Babe, this never ends,

We were never friends.

The harder I try,

For you to not pass by,

In the end, you're unable to comply,

He was never my ally.

You saved, paved, made moments memories,

Held me up, picked me up, gave me remedies.

PERISH.

Feelings that were left unsaid...

Spinning your web around my heart,

Staying trapped in your charm, even if we're miles apart.

Letting myself give in to your kindness forever,

Hiding everything that had to said all together.

All I needed was a little bit of your love,

But you chased me away,

Use me abuse me, take refuge in my arms don't refuse me.

Being different, can't blame you for who you are,

Formless, shapeless like water,

Words can't describe the flow of love that pours within me,

Bring me back a thousand times just to relive this moment again,
dragging you back to hell with me then.

--xxx--

Was it all relatable?

Damn, The Book's over

(is it tho?)

Thank you for reading

XOXO, Abood